Life Goes On..?

Life Goes On..?

A Story of Inspiration.

Jenna Rose Lowthert

"I think about how there are certain people who come into your life and leave a mark. The ones who are as much a part of you as your own soul. Their place in your heart is tender; a bruise of longing, a pulse of unfinished business. Just hearing their name pushes and pulls at you in a hundred different ways, and when you try to define those hundred ways, describe them even to yourself, words are useless. Even if you had a lifetime to talk, there would still be things left unsaid…"

-Sara Zarr

Contents

INTRODUCTION

Life goes on. But does it really?

When my beautiful 47 year old mother, Gina, was diagnosed with stage four Lung Cancer, my world as I knew it came tumbling down. As a 23 year old girl, ready to start a life of my own, this heart wrenching news was more than I could bear.

Together we battled her terminal illness. Along the way we shared happiness, sadness, laughter, love, hope & heartache.

We went through the motions, the ups and the downs. I stood by her side as she inspired many others who were also fighting this beast they call cancer, to keep on fighting. We kept the hope strong as she had an army behind her cheering her on, every step of the way.

When my mom passed away only ten months after her diagnosis I found treasures that she had left behind that told a story of a mother's undying love. Treasures that will forever remain in my mind, body, heart, and soul. Treasures that brought a new hope and profound reason to carry on the life she loved to live so very much.

This true story was written with the intent to inspire many. To those who are fighting the fight, keep on fighting. To those who have experienced tremendous loss, like myself, we must remember that even through the darkest of days, life does in fact go on.

MEMORIAL DAY

It was May 27th 2013, Memorial Day. Any other Memorial Day weekend I would be partying with friends, celebrating life, drink in hand, good music on, and tons of dancing. Not this Memorial Day. I spent all weekend at Morristown Memorial Hospital with my mother. I didn't want to leave her side. Several people came to visit her, my friends, her friends, and family members.

She kept asking me "So what are you doing for Memorial Day? Why aren't you down the shore? Why aren't you out with your friends?" I looked at her and said "Mom, there is nowhere else in the world I would rather be right now than right here with you."

She begged the nurse to let her wash her hair, finally the nurse gave in. My older sister,

Kristina, helped her. Clumps of hair were falling out from the chemotherapy treatments she had a few days prior. She never lost her hair from any chemotherapy treatments before, so this was new to us.

I remember Mom asking "is my hair falling out?" with tears in her eyes. She rarely cried in front of us. She was strong, positive, determined, and had a great will to live. Even with the tears she held back, she still had a smile on her face.

In this moment of sadness, I sat there and stared at the wall, I thought to myself, "How could this be my life? Why me? Why her? What did mom do to deserve this?"

My beautiful 47 year old mother was in the hospital dying from stage 4 non-small cell lung cancer that had spread to her bones.

Yes, she was a smoker, but she had quit four years prior to being diagnosed. What does it matter if she was a smoker? It's still my mother, she's still dying from this terrible disease, and the past can't be changed. Besides, the type of lung cancer she had is found in those of non-smokers.

FLASHBACKS

A few days prior to Mom's diagnosis I remember being on my lunch break at work. It was an absolutely beautiful summer day; I sat alone at the picnic table outside of my job, with a thousand thoughts running through my mind. The unknown was killing me. The sooner I found out, the sooner I could find a way to help her.

I had my music playing and a song came on, the lyrics sang "Cancer don't discriminate, or care if you're just 38, with three kids who need you in their lives…" ("I'm gonna love you through it" Martina McBride) I balled my eyes out for a few minutes, preparing myself for the worst, but tried to convince myself that no matter what the outcome was, everything would be okay.

I went home every night after work and found myself on the internet for hours on end. I researched anything I could find out about lung cancer. The sites read "Lung cancer is the leading cancer killer in both men and women in the United States. In 1987, it surpassed breast cancer to become the leading cause of cancer deaths in women" and the dreaded statistics stated that it was a 1% chance that a person with stage four lung cancer would be alive five years after diagnosis.

"What!? This can't be" I thought to myself. If Mom can't beat the odds, I'll be 29 when she dies. This cannot be possible. How would I go on without her? My mother, my best friend. The only person in this world who knows and understands me completely.

THREE LITTLE WORDS

The dreaded day finally came. July 19th 2012. Dad called me at work and told me to stop by the house on my way home. Tens of thousands of thoughts ran through my mind on my way there. I was about to find out if Mom had terminal cancer or if the spot they found on her lung was benign. I walked in the house, my cousins were there. I already knew what I was about to be told. Mom sat me down and the words poured out of her mouth "I have stage four non-small cell lung cancer that has spread to my bones."

She told me over and over again "Everything is going to be okay. We will get through this. I will fight until the end. I have hope." My whole life as I knew it fell apart in the matter of seconds. Three little words would change everything "I have cancer."

I went home and cried, and cried, and cried some more. Days passed by. Kristina took Mom wig shopping to be prepared for hair loss from the chemotherapy. She got a beautiful wig, which actually looked like her own hair.

Mom was on schedule to start chemotherapy in a week or so, on a Friday. I would be the one to take her every three weeks.

I was so happy to do it; I loved spending time with her. The first chemotherapy session I remember Mom being so scared, but she still continued to smile. One thing that amazed me was how Mom would go into the "chemo room" filled with several other cancer patients and she would try to make conversation with everyone else, tried to make them laugh and smile. She always wanted to spread her love and positivity.

I'll never forget Mom's motto when she was first diagnosed, she would shout "Cancer don't have me! I have cancer." She made some new friends along the way during her chemotherapy sessions, including the nurses. Everyone there loved her, she always made people laugh.

Her strength and courage amazed me that day and it will continue to amaze me for the rest of my life.

A NETWORK OF HOPE

When Mom was first diagnosed I decided to make a Facebook page to update friends on her state of health. Little did we know the amount of love, prayer, and support that would come our way. Mom and I were overwhelmed by it all. With each new post came more and more uplifting comments. More and more people were cheering her on.

I'd like to think Mom has always been a popular woman, known around town as the "cool Mom", she would now be known as the little Italian four foot eleven "tough Mom" who was going to kick cancers ass!

She also started posting on Facebook daily, sharing her journey along with positive thoughts of her own. So many people looked forward to her positive morning posts. Mom wasn't the best writer, or speller for that matter but her posts always put a smile on my face along with several others.

July 23rd, 2012- Four days after Moms diagnosis.

"I have a battle to fight as the weeks go on…I will win this war, that's for sure. I have my wonderful family who are near and far. I have so many people who have my back, especially my husband, who is my rock. I will update you all on this life changing thing they call cancer. I have many tests this week but I won't fear that. My treatments will start but I am ready for them. You might get a call from me; I might need help a bit here and there. I would like to thank everybody for all the awesome posts and support. I am one lucky person. I love you all. Until next week…..that's all folks!"

-Gina Marie Lowthert, Facebook Post.

THE MUSIC OF MY HEART

Mom was never one for slower music. She liked dance music, rock music. Me? I love music with meaning, songs with lyrics that speak to you. So I thought it was odd when Mom started listening to the band Train, who I actually happen to love. Her new theme song was "Calling All Angels". She would always include that in her all of Facebook posts and everybody knew it was "her song".

Mom told me plenty of times that "Calling All Angels" would come on before her scans and she knew she would have good scan results. Almost like a sign from above, a sign from loved ones who have already passed on, letting her know that she's going to be okay.

I've always been skeptical about signs and an afterlife. After all one will never know what happens when you die, until you actually die. Not knowing what was ahead for Mom, I forced myself to believe. Believe that when you do die you eventually are with the ones you love, eternally.

I guess you could say I developed a stronger faith after Mom's diagnosis. So calling all angels it was, and believe me when I say I played that song every day. I was calling any angel that would help us.

Mom completed round one of chemotherapy with flying colors. We made sure to have balloons and cards set up for when Mom got home that day. Kristina and I got her a cute little i-pod that she could listen to during her doctor visits. Come to think of it now, She never even used that thing, she was such a little chatter box.

Every time I was with her I would always try to snap pictures of her, just as memories, and to post to update everyone. She looked great, but she hated getting her picture taken. Even though she was a photographer, she never liked the camera on her.

SUMMERTIME SADNESS

Every summer for a few years now, Mom and Dad would take me and a few of my friends, along with a few of Kristina's friends to Ocean City, Maryland. My poor Dad was stuck with six to eight girls each year.

Mom loved it there. She would rent a nice big condo, we would all go food shopping together, and she made us all dinner each night. We made sure we were stocked with all of the ingredients to make her famous kamikaze shots!

We had nightly dance parties at the condo before going out. I remember the song "Shots" being on, Mom had the shaker in her hand whipping up shots for all. We were smiling, laughing, and singing along.

Because of Mom's cancer, we decided not to go to Ocean City in 2012. "Next year we will go, for sure!" Mom always said. Something about that place had her heart. And now it will forever have mine.

Summer started flying by. We still did our normal family dinners and barbeques. Man did she make the best spaghetti and meatballs every Sunday! It didn't matter if she wasn't feeling well from the chemotherapy; she was determined to make us her famous meatballs. She would spend all Sunday preparing her homemade sauce and getting everything ready for dinner.

Mom would always say to me "You have to learn how to make this, so when I'm not around anymore, you can make it for Dad." I always brushed those little comments off. I was in denial. Mom is going to be around for many more years and she will always make my favorite Sunday meal! Right?

Round two and three of chemotherapy was successful. Mom rarely got sick, or at least she didn't let us know if she wasn't feeling well. She went on with her normal routines. She owned a daycare in her home for many years, which she still continued to do. She also volunteered her time at the local social services in town. She refused to give either of those up.

Mom waited for her hair to fall out. She prepared herself every day, but it never really did. She still had her own beautiful dark brown hair and didn't have to use her wig.

September 19th, 2012

"8 weeks into chemo and yes it's still all my hair!"

-Gina Marie Lowthert, Facebook Post

Eight weeks into chemotherapy and everything seemed to be going very well...

September 30th 2012

"I love when people see me, the look on their face. Yes, I have lung cancer. I feel great and nothing is going to stop me from doing the things I want. CANCER DON'T HAVE ME! I take each day and I live it…just like anyone else. We can all go at any given time. I JUST LIVE LIKE I DON'T HAVE LUNG CANCER. Simple as that. Have a great night everyone. Calling all angels."

-Gina Marie Lowthert, Facebook Post.

DATE WITH MR. CHEMO

Despite the fact that everything seemed to be going well, it still broke my heart to see Mom go through of all this torture. She still had a terminal cancer, she still had pretty bad odds of beating it. Yet she kept on going. Nothing was stopping her and nothing was going to take her away from her family, friends and the life she loved to live.

After all why did this happen to her? But why does it happen to anyone? No one deserves this, no one.

Every three weeks we went to Saint Claire's Oncology center in Denville, NJ. Mom and I made it fun. We sat there for three or more hours or so while the IV dripped into her veins. We talked to other patients there, got to know their stories. It was always so sad seeing the other patients. Most of them didn't look as healthy as Mom did.

September 30th, 2012

"Date with Mr. Chemo today!"

-Gina Marie Lowthert, Facebook Post.

We were driving back from our "date with Mr. Chemo" and Mom insisted on driving. She never did like to get in the car with me behind the wheel. The music was blaring as usual, we would always sing along to the radio or play "name that tune." The song "Daylight" by Adam Levine came on the radio. The lyrics sang "And when the day light comes I'll have to go, but tonight I'm gonna hold you so close…" Mom looked over at me with a little smile on her face and said "I wonder what this song means?" I must have been in a bad mood because I snapped at her "Ugh, who really cares what this stupid song means right now." I answered back in a feisty tone.

Now when I hear that song it's like nails on a chalk board to me. I can't even listen to it without thinking about that day. I wish I talked to her about what I thought it meant because I know she would have shared what she thought it meant, and man now I would love to know.

It is the little moments like this in life that we sometimes get so caught up and take for granted. I know Mom didn't take it to heart, but me? Well now I do.

INSPIRE

There is a website Mom joined called Inspire. It is a cancer support group website, where people shared thoughts, asked questions, and shared information to help each other. I decided to join also so Mom would realize she is not in this alone and never will be. She made friends on there, many friends from all over, people in the same boat as her.

I would log on go on there from time to time and post also, which in turn I made friends with young girls my age whose mothers were also battling this beast they call lung cancer.

My friends have always been there for me, but how would they possibly ever understand what I'm going through? They couldn't and I would never expect them to. I was so desperate for answers. I searched high and low, asked any question I could find. I started to think I could be an Oncologist myself with all the information I was finding out.

After each and every scan Mom had I forced her to get a copy of the written report. I even went as far as getting the actual x-ray image. We had to wait a few days after the actual scan to see the doctor who would then read us the results. I needed immediate answers.

You see, when people with cancer go for any type of scan there's a word they use called "Scaniexty" and honestly I think my "Scaniexty" was worse than Mom's.

Who did I think I was? I am no doctor, I cannot read x-rays. I was desperate, desperate to cure her, desperate to have my healthy, beautiful mother back.

September 19th 2012- "PLEASE, PLEASE HELP ME TRANSLATE THIS

SCAN!!! My Mom has stage four lung cancer with metastasis to ribs, hip and tailbone. She was diagnosed July 19th. She has so far had 2 rounds of chemotherapy. Her mass was in her upper left lobe. She had her CT scan last week and we got the results printed before our doctor visit this Friday (We are very impatient!)

The results read:

"This CT scan was compared to PET scan on July 25th 2012. FINDINGS- There has been dramatic improvement in a left upper lobe mass, with near complete resolution of mediastinal and hilar adenopathy. The majority of the adenopathy resides in the left hilar and sub cardinal locations. A dominant Subcarinal node measures 1.6 cm in transverse dimension, node was previously 3.4 cm. The great vessels are normal in course and caliber. The lungs demonstrate no evidence of infiltrate or effusion. Sclerotic bony lesions are seen in the 8th and 4th rib on the right. There has been interval sclerosis of the left sixth transverse process metastasis. Upper abdominal images are unremarkable.

IMPRESSION: Marked positive response to known left upper lobe mass and extensive adenopathy."

*That was a post I had posted on the Inspire website. It gives an idea of just how _desperate_ I was.

BETTER DAYS AHEAD

Well, her scan results in September were great! Excellent news as a matter of fact! Her tumor was nearly GONE! I couldn't believe it. We were so happy. That may have been one of the best days of my life.

Things were looking up. Maybe there is a chance for her, and maybe she is going to beat the odds! Maybe Mom will be here to see me get married, have kids, and buy a house. You know, all of the exciting things that start happening when you're a 23 year old girl ready to go out into the "big girl world" all on your own. But I didn't want to be on my own. I wanted to be with Mom. All of my focus was on her. My new life mission was to get her well. I have always been a social butterfly, I've always loved going out, and I guess I got that from Mom. She was the exact same way. After her diagnosis my life pretty much stopped. I dedicated a lot of time to helping her. And I wouldn't change that for anything.

We heard of a local lung cancer walk in town and we decided to go. Kristina raised money to donate to the walk. A large group of us went, along with Mom. We walked three miles and amazingly Mom pretty much walked the whole way. They played music, paid tribute to the survivors, it was a beautiful day. All of the survivors wore a green shirt. When they called the survivors up on stage, Mom ran up there. I could tell how happy she was to still be here with us and how she was so proud that she was a survivor.

Our team name was "Gina's Angels." But in reality, she was my angel; she has always been my angel.

October 20th 2012

"Doctor's visit was good. Blood work good. She asked me if I was even doing chemo. Lol, she said there are a handful of people on chemo that are doing as well as I am. Things are looking good. I thank everyone that sends me good thoughts. Love to all. I AM BLESSED"

-Gina Marie Lowthert, Facebook Post.

After hearing the great news of Mom's scan, I remember being at my house where I lived with my boyfriend at the time. I was watching television and something popped up.

It was the band Train's documentary, get to know the band. I immediately called Mom and told her to turn it on.

Ironically, Train has a song called "Drops of Jupiter", which I found out while watching the show that the lead singer, Pat Monahan, actually wrote for his Mom who had passed away from lung cancer. In the show he explained the meaning behind the song, stating that he had a dream about her after she died, floating in the atmosphere and wrote a song about it. I was shocked because I always thought that song had a completely different meaning to it. "Now tell me did the wind sweep you off your feet, did you finally get the chance to dance along the light of day & head back to the Milky Way, to see the lights all faded, and that heaven is overrated."

Now Mom decided when she hears this song it has bad meaning behind it. So I never played it around her. But I started hearing it a lot more.

There are certain memories that stick out in my mind that I don't think I will ever forget. Not now, not in 20 years from now, maybe not ever. This song is one of them. But we still called all angels.

October 26th, 2012

"Awesome PET scan!!!! Thank you to all who think of me. Life is good! Calling all angels <3"

-Gina Marie Lowthert, Facebook Post.

STORMS OF LIFE

The end of October was near; a bad storm was headed our way. They called it "Super Storm Sandy" and "Sandy" was raging up the coast of New Jersey, leaving pretty much everybody without power for weeks.

I decided to spend that week with my parents. Everybody was a bit on edge, between no power, no heat, no hot water, no TV, pretty much like living in the Stone Age.

Still no power when October 30th came around. Mom's 48th birthday! Yes on mischief night, she was a little mystery herself. She never wanted to do much for her birthday, and this year there wasn't much to do because of the storm. But like usual all she wanted was to be with her family.

Mom wasn't one to go over the top and never expected gifts. She would always say "Don't get me anything! Save your money!" She made me laugh when she said that. She absolutely hated when people spent any money on her. But how could I not get her something? Of course I was getting her something. I bought her a beautiful gold necklace that said "Hope." She wore it every day.

That Friday we were heading into New York City, to go see a doctor at Sloane Kettering Cancer Center to get a second opinion and to see if Mom was on the right track. After all, they are known to be one of the best cancer centers in America. We could spend the day in the city, get lunch, get good news from the doctor then head home.

I remember clear as day waking up that morning in a bad mood. I fought with Mom and said some things I don't want to repeat. I'll never forget her going into the living room, she sat down and cried. I felt horrible and started crying myself. I hated that moment and still hate it to this day. But of course being the best person she could be, she hugged me and we went on with our day.

Me, Kristina, Mom, and Dad headed into the city. We had an adventurous little hour car ride there. We grabbed lunch, heard from the doctor at Sloane Kettering that she was, in fact, on the right track and everything seemed to be looking great.

We headed back home later that day. The car ride home was hilarious; we laughed the whole way home. Traffic was terrible due to the storm damage. But it was a wonderful car ride, filled with family bonding, laughter and love. One I will never forget.

November 7th 2012

"Got Power? I do! Yahoo!"

-Gina Marie Lowthert, Facebook Post

After several days without power, it was finally restored!

HOPE RINGS ETERNAL

November arrived and Mom was doing great. She looked beautiful as always. She still had the same amazing spirit along with her own hair.

We celebrated Thanksgiving. Mom made a remark at dinner "This may be my last Thanksgiving with you guys!" then giggled. I hated when she said stuff like that. But maybe it was her way of coping with the situation. Though she made it into a joke, I don't think she was joking. Even though her scan results were pretty good, lung cancer, especially stage four, is very sneaky. It can be gone and back within weeks. We weren't in the clear yet. She wasn't able to say she was NED (no evidence of disease). I waited to hear NED, that's all I wanted to hear was NED!

Like any other person, we don't ever know what tomorrow will bring. No one can predict the future and no one knows when their time on earth will end. I think cancer has a way of messing with your head. In the back of Mom's mind, I knew she knew what the outcome would eventually be. I was in denial. I didn't want to even believe that she was living with stage four lung cancer, but she was. And she continued to live her life the way she wanted to.

November 16th, 2012

"Today is Mom's 6th and last round of chemotherapy! Four months ago she was diagnosed with stage four lung cancer. Looking at her now you would never know she even has cancer. Her cancer may never be gone, but with her amazing response to treatment and all the love around her, she is winning this battle so far!! So thankful that we have been this lucky and so thankful for all of the support and love from you all <3 love you Mom! You are a fighter!"

-Post from my Facebook.

Mom rang the bell outside of the cancer center today! It was a beautiful moment. Dad and I were there to see. She was so happy. She cried happy tears, tears of joy. I gave her a big hug and told her how much I loved her and that she was doing so well with everything. I was so proud of her.

November 30th, 2012

"Went to the doctors, blood work all good. Won't start chemo maintenance until 2013. She said I'm doing awesome! Thank you everyone for always asking me how I am doing and thank you for all the prayers and love. I love you all. Have an awesome weekend everyone."

Gina Marie Lowthert, Facebook Post.

A WHITE CHRISTMAS

November came and went, one more month down. Mom was now a five month lung cancer survivor! Yeah, five months doesn't seem like a lot. But I was counting the days, even minutes that she was a survivor. Every second mattered to me.

Christmas was quickly approaching, Mom put up her cute little tree. It was decorated so nicely in her favorite colors, deep purple and silver.

Every Christmas had been pretty much the same for years, simple. Our family is very simple. We have a very small family. Just Mom, Dad, Kristina, Dawn, Dawn was not only Mom's cousin but more like a sister to her, a best friend. Mom always said Dawn was her angel. Then there is Dawn's husband Joe and their daughter Danielle who is my cousin but just like Mom and Dawn, Danielle is more like a second sister to me. Lastly there is my grandmother, Rosie and my Uncle Jimmy. Two crazy Italians, but they always make family gatherings extra fun.

We all were together on Christmas Eve, dancing around to Italian Christmas songs; "Dominick the Donkey" has always been one of our personal favorites! We made little homemade pizzas, drank a little of course and enjoyed the night.

Again Mom said "This is going to be my last Christmas with you guys!" and giggled. For someone who was so positive, I hated hearing her say that. "No Mom" I said. "It is not going to be your last Christmas with us, hate to break it to you!" and we all laughed.

Christmas morning came. I spent the day with Mom, Dad, Kristina, and my grandma. Mom gave me and Kristina each a little keepsake box. It had a note in there and a few other childhood memories. I knew why she did that. She wanted us to treasure those moments forever and she never wanted us to forget how much she loved us, which she did so very much.

Mom gave me, Kristina, and Danielle each a necklace. She said it meant the power of three, and she wanted us to always stick together. We found out later that she actually made up the fact that the necklaces meant power of three. We all got a good laugh out of it. I got Mom an angel statue that said "Every day is a gift, every year a new beginning." I also got her a nice cancer ribbon necklace with white diamonds in it. I remember being at the store and picking it out and the lady saying to me, "But honey it's not pink, is this the one you really want?" I said "I don't want a pink one I want a white one." she looked at me in confusion. Yes lady, not all cancer is pink! For the love of god, the lung cancer ribbon is white! Not that I expected her to know that because if Mom didn't have lung cancer I probably wouldn't know that either. But like I said, not all cancer is pink.

I used to get mad when people compared Mom's cancer to breast cancer, or any other type of cancer for that matter. Lung cancer is the number one cancer killer. Why doesn't anyone know or understand this?

I took a step back and remember telling myself "Don't be like that, don't get mad, people don't understand, and every single persons situation is different."

Later that week I found a quote online it read "What is the worst type of cancer? The type that you or someone you love is unfortunate to have." And my whole outlook changed. That is true. Cancer sucks. All cancers suck. And I decided that from that day on, I will not compare cancers. Instead I will do my best to help find a cure for all types.

SHE TALKS TO ANGELS

I've always loved music. Towards the end of 2012, I decided I wanted to start playing the acoustic guitar. My parents bought me one and I was so excited to learn. I would go to my parent's house and practice with Dad every Sunday.

The first song I tried learning was "She talks to angels" by The Black Crowes. I tried and tried, knowing eventually I would get it right. One day.

The way Mom looked at me as I practiced and got a little better each time gave me a sense of sadness. I knew she was happy that I was trying and learning but I felt as if she knew she may not be here to see me play when I actually get really good.

I could see it in her eyes how so very proud of me she was, not only for learning the guitar but for the woman I was becoming. The woman she raised.

I tried to ignore the fact that I got that sense when I looked at her, almost as if I was in denial, that in all honesty she most likely wouldn't be here to see me get really good at the guitar. Would she even be here next year? I wasn't sure. But I never gave up hope.

NEW BEGINNINGS

Christmas was over, now we must make plans for my favorite holiday ever. New Year's Eve! Since I was little I have never spent a New Year's Eve without Mom. Once I turned 21 I was sure that she would be partying with me. I could never leave my fun mom out, she was the life of the party; even my friends wanted her there.

We all planned to go to a local open bar and get hotel rooms so we could all be together. That night was one of the best nights. There were about 15 of us. Mom had the time of her life! We smiled, cried, laughed, danced, and drank night away!

December 30th, 2012

"So 2013 is right around the corner. Okay so we are all going to give up something, go on a diet, exercise, eat better….blah, blah, blah- I won't give up anything. Life is too short. I will enjoy every day like it's my last. I wish all if my family and friends the best 2013 ever. Love to all<3"

-Gina Marie Lowthert, Facebook Post.

I loved that post. It made me laugh; I look back every now and then and read through her posts, they were always so funny and uplifting. I wish I had a way to express how many people she actually inspired every single day. She was so selfless and selfless is an understatement.

Even while she was sick, she would always help people in any way she could. I could say it over and over again and I still wouldn't have the right words to describe what an amazing person she was.

With 2012 coming to an end, I could honestly say it was a pretty bad year. I sat home one night with my soft music playing and reflected on the year and how much my life has changed.

In just six short months my whole life was different. Mostly in a bad way, yes, but I noticed I was changing into a better person, changing into the beautiful person Mom was.

WHAT CANCER CANNOT DO

2013 was here! With the New Year came new hope, new faith, and hopefully good health for Mom. We hadn't been to the oncologist since the beginning of December. Mom had a scheduled appointment for some time in the beginning of January. We went to the doctor's office; in a weird way I could tell Mom was excited to see her oncologist and all of the nurses. They had a sign hanging in the office, it read..

"What Cancer Cannot Do"

Cancer is so limited...
It cannot cripple love.
It cannot shatter hope.
It cannot corrode faith.
It cannot eat away peace.
It cannot destroy confidence.
It cannot kill friendship.
It cannot shut out memories.
It cannot silence courage.
It cannot reduce eternal life.
It cannot quench the Spirit.

I loved that sign. It's so true; cancer may be able to end a life but it cannot take away unconditional love.

The nurse called us into the doctor's office. The office was pretty busy that day; we waited a while for the doctor to come in. Dad snapped this great photo of me and mom.

We finally sat down with the oncologist and went over her last scan, she was stable! She wasn't cancer free but she was stable! Sounds great to me! We were so happy.

But Mom was having bad back pain; she would always say "It's just muscle pain from the way I sleep." She always had an excuse. I don't know if she just said that because she didn't want to worry me, or because she was trying to convince herself that the pain wasn't from the cancer.

January 23rd, 2013

"Word on the street is… I AM STABLE!"

-Gina Marie Lowthert, Facebook Post

After hearing the great news that Mom was stable, the doctor was still concerned about her back. She sent Mom for an MRI.

A Week or so later the MRI results showed that a tumor in fact was now growing on her spine, along with the one in her lung. How could this have happened so fast? I didn't understand cancer then and I still don't understand it now. I asked why they couldn't do surgery. The location of the tumor was the reason.

I accepted this upsetting news and I figured that if her 1st line of chemotherapy has failed her, the second one may work and bring her to NED (no evidence of disease.) Let's give it a shot! They even suggested radiation, which she did. She was going to be starting a new chemotherapy, this one was in pill form. It was Called Tarceva. I read a lot about it and many of people have had good results from it.

I was excited for her to start her new treatment. Mom was very hopeful. After all, she was feeling great, had all her hair, and she looked beautiful as always. HOPE. We never gave up hope.

FUNNY VALENTINE

It was Valentine's Day; I was at work. I decided I was going to get a tattoo for Mom. I was so excited; I went on my lunch break from work. I got a very simple lung cancer ribbon tattooed on my right hands ring finger.

The tattoo artist asked me "Do you want me to color the ribbon in pink?" I didn't get aggravated; it actually didn't bother me this time. I went on and explained to her that Mom has lung cancer, not breast cancer and that the lung cancer ribbon is white. I figured the more people I could educate on lung cancer, the more people who will be aware.

She was shocked when I told her how old Mom. Maybe if more people knew that age doesn't play a factor in this disease, more people can be saved.

I went back to work, showed off my new tattoo and I sent Mom a picture of me making a punching fist showing the new tattoo "Hurt like hell, but this one's for you mama!, now let's kick cancers ass." she thought I was crazy, she laughed but I know she loved it.

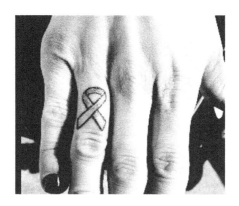

ENDLESS LOVE

March flew by, Mom was still on her chemotherapy pill, she did okay with radiation. She seemed to be doing alright. Okay, maybe I noticed she wasn't doing as well as last year, but she still had her positive spirit and hope for the future.

April 9th, 2013

"When you wake this morning and your feet hit the floor, think about how lucky you are. Yes little things get in the way, but 98% of the time and most can be fixed. For me, I thank god that I still get up every day, I can still do all this things I love. I get to see and hear my family and friends. I might be living with cancer but it won't change a thing about life and how good it is. Be thankful of everything that comes your way today. A smile from someone, finding a penny heads up, saying thank you, or even just seeing a tiny flower in bloom. LIFE IS GOOD AND I AM BLESSED. CALLING ALL ANGELS. Have a good day love to all."

-Gina Marie Lowthert, Facebook Post.

This is another one of my favorite posts of mom's. She was simply amazing.

Mom and Dad's 28th wedding anniversary was near. April 13th. My parents had a love that was real. Sometimes you see people grow old together but at the same time they grow apart. Life gets so busy sometimes; I think more people need to stop and smell the roses. After all that is what kept my parents happy for 28 years.

I was so glad Mom was well enough to celebrate their anniversary. Dad got Mom a beautiful globe with an angel in it. "Gina, My Love, My Life. Happy 28th Anniversary." Was engraved in it.

April 13th 2013

"28 years ago I married the man of my dreams. We started out as friends and became husband and wife. My best friend, who I love so very much. He is my rock, my life, my hero. We have had our share of hard times over the years but always made it through. This last one is a big one and what didn't kill us will make us stronger. When I see he is face every morning I think how luck can I be? I say I am very, very, lucky. I love you with everything I have. We both have been blessed with so many people in our lives and we thank you all for always being there for us... I love you always and forever."

-Gina Marie Lowthert, Facebook Post.

Later on that month, Mom wanted to have a family outing. She decided we were all going to go to the local casino for dinner and a fun night of gambling. After all Mom did love to gamble.

I could remember when I was younger; probably around age 15 or 16, Mom would always buy the scratch off lottery tickets. We would do them together. Most of the time we lost, but we still always had fun doing it. I could hear Mom's voice saying "I can't wait until you're 21 so we can go to the casino together!"

There were about 15 of us, we met at the casino and ate dinner together. Mom was so excited about the huge buffet, but her favorite was the crab legs. We finished dinner and all went out on the floor to start our gambling. Mom was crazy when she gambled. She was all over the place; most of us couldn't keep up with her. She would hop from one slot machine to the next in hopes of hitting big.

That was the last time we were all together. I remember how much fun she had and how glad she was that we all went together.

A TURN FOR THE WORSE

It was some time towards the end of April. Things were taking a turn for the worst. Mom spiked a fever and it was very hard for her to breathe. Dad took her to the Hospital. She really wasn't doing well. They admitted her to the hospital where she would stay on the "Simon 5" Cancer unit.

I wasn't sure at the time what was going on. It all happened very, very fast. She was pretty sick, in a lot of pain and she didn't look like her normal self. But still, Mom kept that positive spirit of hers alive.

Days had passed, Mom was still at the hospital. I was wondering when the heck they were going to let her go home. She got so many prayers and so much support it was unbelievable. One of the nurses even had to tell us to keep our voices down in the room because she had too many visitors. It was endless. One visitor would leave and the next would show up.

My family being the way we are, joked and laugh a lot. We tried to keep Mom comfortable and make her feel at home. She wanted me to spend the night at the hospital with her, so I did. I remember being on the little fold out bed next to her, she was coughing and moaning in pain all night long. I got up to ask her if she was okay. She whispered "Jen, I'm fine, go back to sleep. I love you." I couldn't get back to sleep. But I pretended that I did. I had a silent cry to myself praying she wouldn't hear me. I didn't want her to know I was sad. I knew that would break her heart.

I woke up the next morning, put a little make-up on, got dressed, and spent the day with Mom. We waited for the doctors to come in with some news. After all, it had been a few days and we still didn't know what was going on.

The doctor came in and told Mom that she had a lot of fluid in her lungs, & fluid was building up around her heart. I looked at her and tears came streaming down her face. "So what are we going to do? What's the next step?" she looked at me and cried. The sadness in her eyes was heart breaking. She cried out "This is it Jen, this is my last year with you guys." Her positive spirit was crushed. I tried holding back my tears and told her everything was going to be okay.

A day or two passed and we still had no treatment plan. We asked for answers, but seemed to get nowhere. I had already taken off so many days from work so I decided I would go back for a day and see how I felt. I was at work; I work at a dental office where I had been working there 7 years. I call my co-workers my work family, my second family, because that is what they are to me.

It wasn't even noon. I was pretty busy when my office manager came up to me and said "Jenna, let's go, we are going to the hospital." My heart sank. I knew something wasn't right. Kristina had called her from the hospital and told her to bring me there. I was screaming in the car "What the hell is going on? What happened?" She just answered "Your sister called, we just need to go see your mom." We both started to cry. I cried my eyes out and kept screaming "This is it, isn't it? She's dying; she's going to die, isn't she?! What the hell, I am not ready for this."

We cried together the whole 20 minute drive to the hospital. Mom knew Stacey for a while now; she always told me that Stacey was put in my life for a reason, almost like a second Mom to me. My Mom was so thankful for her.

When we got there everyone was so calm. Kristina pulled me aside and explained to me that the doctors told my family that Mom had about a month left to live. I looked at Mom. She just said to me "Come here, come give me a hug." I jumped into her small hospital bed with her and I hugged her with all my might. Tears rolled down my face. Mom wiped them away and told me not to worry. How could I not worry? I was just told my Mom has a month left to live.

A day passed, we all sat in the hospital from morning until night. It was pretty depressing, but somehow, even though she was in so much pain, Mom made it funny. Like usual her uplifting spirit and energy gave us a little glimpse of hope. Now that I think about it I'm not too sure she really even knew what was going on.

\

FIX YOU

I recall driving back from the hospital after visiting my mom on a rainy spring day in April of 2013. She was so sick, she was in so much pain, she was dying from stage four lung cancer, and she was just 48 years old. A night mare was unfolding right before my eyes.

As I drove, a song came on the radio. I've heard it before and have always liked the tune. But this time the lyrics had personal meaning to me. The radio sang loudly "lights will guide you home, and ignite your bones and I will try to fix you." (Cold Play-Fix You) I immediately started balling my big brown eyes out. I pulled my car over to the side of the road. I was so angry, so angry that my mom had cancer, so angry that my mom was so sick. For once I let negativity get to me. I couldn't think of anything else besides the fact that I was going to lose her. It was inevitable, there was nothing more I could do to help her. That's what I was trying so desperately to do. I was trying to fix her. But she wasn't the broken one. She was so strong, so brave. There was nothing about her that I could fix. Besides having a terminal cancer- she lived a perfect life, she was a perfect person- kind, simple, and content. She knew she was going to be leaving this beautiful world soon and she knew exactly what she would leave behind, but still she smiled and loved me with all she had left in her. It was I who needed the fixing. At just 24 years old my whole world was falling apart right in front of my eyes. My mother, my best friend, the only person who knew and understood me completely was about to be ripped away from me in one of the most horrible ways possible.

I believe that we sometimes have these moments in life, that no matter how long ago, we remember so vividly. As if it were just yesterday. I'm not so sure if it's a good thing or a bad thing. Maybe it's our minds way of taking a picture. Maybe these moments aren't supposed to be forgotten. Maybe they are meant to help you along the journey of healing. After all, without sadness, one would never know what happiness truly is.

HOPE IN SIGHT

A few more heart wrenching days went by. Each day was one day closer to the doctors predicted time of Mom's death. Though the doctors did not want to perform surgery on a stage four lung cancer patient because of the risk, they finally agreed to drain the fluid from her heart and lungs. It was the best news I had heard in a while.

They apologized for telling us she only had a month left to live and explained to us that the fluid could build back up, but it wasn't likely. Surgery was scheduled for 6am the next morning. Mom told me to go home and get some rest and be ready for tomorrow. I told Mom I loved her, and left the hospital.

Ahh yes, a nice quiet car ride home, alone. A million thoughts raced through my mind. What if she doesn't make it through surgery? What if the surgery doesn't work? Before I knew it I was in a car accident. My brand new Camaro, which I worked so hard to get, was destroyed. I immediately called Dad crying. The car accident wasn't my fault. But how many bad things can happen to a person at once?

Mom was too sick to know what was happening. If this happened any other time she would have been calling my cell phone nonstop and racing to the scene of the accident. But instead, I barley heard from her. It upset me, I know how badly she wanted to be there for me, and she was always so worried about me. Like every loving mother is with their children. But she just couldn't be there. I would now have a rental car until my car was repaired.

SECOND CHANCES

Surgery went well. Mom did great. I was so happy she was back on the road to recovery. She would have to stay in the hospital for a few days to recover, but would be coming home soon.

She called me and told me she wanted an egg roll. I said "That's it? Just an egg roll?" she said "Yup. See you soon, love you" so I got the egg roll and got to the hospital. The smile on her face when I gave her the egg roll was priceless.

She was in the unit for patients recovering from the same surgery she had. There was a young man in there, two rooms down. He was around my age. Of course Mom, in her motherly ways, had to make friends with him and see how he was doing. She felt so bad for him so she took one of her own get well balloons, walked herself down the hallway with her oxygen tank behind her, and gave him the balloon. He smiled at her and thanked her. You could tell she made his day.

The next day or so I remember being with Mom, she wanted to walk around a bit, so we decided we were going to pretend that the hospital hallways were a park. We walked down one hall way into another, there hung a big painted picture, and it reminded me of the zoo. I said to Mom "We are no longer in the park ma, we are now entering the zoo!" she looked at me and laughed.

Later that night, Mom had a bunch of visitors. So many, they once again had to tell us to keep quiet. Mom wanted to go for another stroll, but this time with everybody. As we all walked down the hall way I managed to snap a great picture, and I decided that every one of

Mom's friends and family would now be called "Gina's Army." So Gina's army went on a stroll to check out the zoo me and Mom visited earlier that day.

May 6th, 2013

"Hello from Morristown Hospital. Not sure how long I've been here but it's ok. I get a second chance at life. One minute you have 6 weeks to live, the next you're good to go. Please take nothing for granted. You all have been so great to my family and me. I love you all. Now I really need a damn drink. Enjoy the simple things. Smile it will make someone else happy. Have a good day. Xoxox."

-Gina Marie Lowthert, Facebook Post.

Later on, she sent me a video message from the hospital. She had a smile on her face and she said

"Hey Jen, I love you so much. Mama's coming home! I got a second chance at life" she looked so cute in that video. I loved it and watched it over and over again.

She was released from the hospital the next day.

HOME SWEET HOME

Mom was finally home after spending two weeks in the hospital. She could breathe better, but the tumor on her back was still causing her so much pain. She wanted surgery so bad, but it just wasn't possible. She remained so positive and she kept saying how thankful she was that she got a second chance at life. She was on morphine because of the back pain, and was a little out of it most of that week.

It was the middle of the week; I couldn't wait for the week to end so I could spend the weekend and Mother's Day with Mom. I was at work; we had a staff meeting on schedule that day. I sat there in a daze as my boss talked about work concerns. She went behind the desk and grabbed a box; I had no clue what it was. She started to get teary eyed; I then noticed that the box had pictures of me and

Mom on it. She explained to me that the whole office contributed and donated money for Mom to do whatever she wished with.

I was in shock. I know my co-workers are my second family, but they really didn't have to do that. It was such a kind gesture and it truly made me smile, especially because I was having such a hard month.

I went to Mom's on my lunch break to show her. She was still pretty out of it from all of the morphine. I explained to her that my co-workers raised money for her. She was so happy and so thankful. I remember she started crying because she couldn't believe how loved she truly was. Not just by my work family, but by so many others who sent her flowers, balloons, cards, and prayers. In that moment I couldn't believe that Mom was so selfless, selfless enough to the point that she didn't even realize how much she truly touched so many people's lives, in so many different ways.

Why wasn't I like that? I remember thinking to myself, am I selfish? Do I not realize how blessed I truly am? And from that day on I made a promise to myself, that when I am in put in a situation where I can help someone else in need, I will no longer turn a blind eye to it. I will help as much as I can.

MOTHER'S DAY

It was May 12th, 2013, Mother's Day. It was a gorgeous spring day. Somehow Mom gathered the energy and strength to make everybody a home cooked dinner. She set up tables outside so we could all eat together under the gorgeous sky.

But still, she was so out of it from the pain and the morphine. She didn't talk much, but didn't complain once. She served everybody dinner, it was delicious as always. We all talked and tried to make her laugh. I know how glad she was that everybody was together. And I was so glad that she was still here with us.

I thought to myself a few times, could this be my last Mother's Day with Mom? But I quickly snapped out of it. Of course she will be here next year! She's a fighter and she's going to fight until she can't fight anymore!

It was around Mother's Day weekend when I heard that Mom's favorite band Train, would be performing a concert nearby. I told Mom I was going to take her as her Mother's Day gift. She was so excited. After all "Calling all angels" was her song and I knew had bad she wanted to go.

The concert wasn't until July and I knew Mom wasn't doing well, but I was still very hopeful that she would be there with me singing along to the lyrics of her very own favorite song.

MORE OBSTACLES AHEAD

It was a few days after Mother's Day; Mom had a follow up appointment with the surgeon to make sure everything was healing the way it was supposed to. Mom's cousin Dawn took her to the appointment. The visit went fairly well, until the surgeon told her to go to the hospital because her left lung was only receiving 50-70 percent of oxygen.

Dawn called me at work and told me the news. I left work only to have to wait in the emergency room with Mom for hours. She couldn't breathe well, yet they still made her sit in the waiting room. She, herself, had to ask them for an oxygen tank. I was getting very frustrated when finally at about 10pm they did an exam and admitted her back to the same Simon 5 cancer unit she was on the last time she got stuck there. She seemed to be in good spirits and still very positive. I stayed with her until about 1am, and returned back in the morning to spend the day with her.

Little did I know that this was the beginning of the end. Little did I know that in a matter of days my whole world would be changed, forever. Almost the way it changed when I first heard Mom say "I have cancer." But this time it was different. It was a different kind of change. A change that I could never forget. A change that would crush me and break my heart into a million pieces. Never to be repaired again.

LET IT BE

I returned back to the hospital the next morning, only to find Mom in very bad shape. She was in massive amounts of pain, wasn't breathing very well, and didn't want to eat much. I stayed with her all day. An old friend of Mom's had stopped by to visit. She really wasn't up for any visitor, that's how I knew she really didn't feel well. But that still didn't stop them from coming. Once again the overwhelming amount of people checking up on her was amazing.

A day or so went by when her lung doctor came in and told us that it wasn't looking good. He explained to us that her left lung was completely collapsed, and the tumor was pushing into the lobe of her right lung. I didn't understand. Or maybe I didn't want to believe it. How did this all happen so fast?

The doctor pulled up her latest chest scan and showed us. I still denied it. There had to be something they could do for her. ANYTHING. I even begged the doctor to try a surgery on her. He refused and told me there's no possible way they could do surgery on a patient in that condition.

The next day I was with my best friend Joelle, she wanted to come see Mom at the hospital. After all she was almost as close with my own mother as I was.

We were on our way to the hospital when I turned the car around and pulled into the tattoo shop. I don't know what came over me that day, but I decided to get a tattoo on my wrist. It was a quote that said "Let it be" with doves flying around it.

Later that afternoon, Joelle and I showed up at the hospital. Mom was having an okay day. Some days she seemed alright and other days were horrible. Mom, Dad, Dawn, and Kristina were there. I showed Mom the tattoo. She said "Geez Jen, enough with those damn tattoos already." But to me it had meaning. I knew in the back of my mind what was coming. And I knew whatever was coming; I had to let it be.

Joelle spent some time with us and left the hospital. It was now just me, Mom, Dad, Kristina, and Dawn. We were all chatting when Mom interrupted us and went around the room explaining to each one of us what we meant to her and how much she loved us. I can't remember exactly what she said to each one of us, but I do remember her looking at me and saying "You're just my whole world and I love you so much." I got teary eyed and said "Mom, come on stop!" I hated being in situations like that, it was almost like she was trying to say goodbye, without actually saying goodbye.

A LETTER TO GINA

I had the same routine. Each day I would get up in the morning, call Mom at the hospital to see if she wanted me to bring her lunch. It depended on how she was feeling, but most of the time I brought it anyway. I would go to the hospital and sit there with Mom from morning until night. Most of the time she was asleep, or in so much pain she couldn't even talk. But there were a few good days too.

Dad had been at the hospital alone with Mom for a little while. I got a picture message from Mom, it was a letter Dad had written to her.

The letter read-

"A letter to Gina, one of the most loving, caring, & giving people I've ever known.. The loving mother of my beautiful girls. A caring daughter. A beautiful, loving wife- the love of my life. Always willing to listen to other people's problems and never speaking of her own. Always has a positive attitude. Always encouraging and thinking of others before herself. One of the best cooks in the word! Excellent home maker – always keeping things going around the house, running her day care business, cleaning, cooking, laundry, shopping…all the things I find hard to do. Provided loving daycare for well over a hundred children- most who she's still in contact with- They all love you! You asked me to never forget you- How could I when you are my heart, my soul, my reason to live. I love you more."

I finally showed up at the hospital, later that afternoon. Mom wasn't feeling too great. It was the same routine, dinner arrived, she tried to eat a little, and I would help her up occasionally to go to the bathroom. Despite all of the sadness in Mom's hospital room, we still all found reasons to laugh and share love, even Mom.

Mom's back pain was out of control at this point so her doctors decided to put her on a morphine drip. Mom always said when Dad put his hand on the spot of her back that hurt, it made her feel better for a Moment . So she would always ask him to sit on the bed and press his hand on her back, with a look of relief on her face. Mom and Dad were sitting together on the bed when I managed to capture a sad yet beautiful picture on my phone and I remember thinking to myself, "this is what love is. Their love is unconditional; this is what life is all about.

TIME

It was Thursday, May 23rd 2013. I called Mom in the morning and she shockingly sounded great. I decided I was going to go to work for a little and would visit Mom later in the day. After all I really needed a break, that hospital was so sad, especially the cancer unit.

I remember getting to work around 8 am; something told me that I needed to be with Mom. I left work and rushed to the hospital. When I arrived Mom was up and walking, she was very talkative, she was even eating a full lunch. I was so happy. I saw a huge glimpse of hope.

This day, although Mom seemed great, is a day I will never forget. It was the day the floor doctor told us it was time to put Mom on hospice. WHAT? HOSPICE? That didn't even cross my mind. I knew Mom wasn't doing well, but they just started in hospital chemotherapy treatments a few days prior. This must be a mistake.

I didn't tell Mom about the hospice, but she somehow put two and two together and figured it out. One of her best childhood friends, Crystal, was in the room when the doctor came in to check on Mom. Mom was very spunky that day so hospice being brought up was very confusing to me. Without the doctor saying a word Mom said to him. "Listen here doc, I don't know what everyone thinks is going on here, but I am not going on hospice. I am not dying, and if I was dying, I wouldn't be here! I would be dancing on a bar somewhere with an IV of vodka in my arm instead of this crap!" The doctor looked at her in awe, and before he could get a word out Mom said "Now no more negative Nancy's in my room please!" The doctor was in shock but had a smirk on his face and said to Mom "Gina, you are amazing" and walked right out of the room.

We all laughed. Crystal and I looked at each other and shook our heads. We weren't surprised that my Mom basically told the doctor off. After all she was a fighter, she wasn't giving up on herself and she wasn't going to let anyone else give up on her.

Later that day we went for a walk around the hospital floor. I was amazed at how much Mom walked around, with her oxygen tank behind her. She didn't want any help either. She was doing it all on her own. That brave woman. When we finally got to the end of the hallway where there was a family waiting room, Mom looked at me and said "Want a coffee? I'll make you one."

The last photo ever taken with my mom.

Dad later arrived at the hospital, only to find the nurses and doctor ready to have a meeting with us to discuss hospice. I begged and begged for them to find some way to help her. They said there was nothing more that they could do.

That's when I decided that I was not going to take no for an answer. No was not an option to me when it came to my mother. I was going to try to save her life, just like I had been trying to for the last ten months.

I went to the hospitals x-ray center, gathered all of her records and immediately rushed them to Sloan Kettering Cancer Center in NYC. The doctor at Sloane Kettering got in touch with us and said he would accept her case as long as she could make it into the city without an ambulance bringing her. She had to be well enough to leave the hospital and travel an hour with us by car. We scrambled any bit of information we could get together, had the nurses set us up with enough oxygen for the car ride.

I went home that night, so excited that they were going to take her case. I packed a bag of clothes and stuff I would need just in case we were going to spend the night in the city. I went to bed with relief and a great sense of hope for tomorrow.

WHEN IT RAINS

It was now Friday May 24th, 2013, Memorial Day weekend. I arrived at the hospital very early that morning, along with Dad and Kristina. We had the car packed and ready to go, but there was one problem. Mom spiked a fever and her blood pressure was rising, so the doctor wouldn't release her. That saying when it rains, it pours pretty much described our luck so far.

I remember getting so frustrated and angry, I couldn't even make eye contact with the nurses or doctors. This was my one chance to try to save her and now its Memorial Day weekend, they won't do transfers tomorrow on a Saturday, or a Sunday, or on actual Memorial Day for that matter. I was so angry. Angry might have been an understatement but Mom really wasn't feeling well so I had to focus my energy on making her feel better. Being it was Memorial Day weekend the doctors agreed to stop trying to send Mom home on hospice. Dad wasn't sure how she would do at home. How would he give her the morphine drip all on his own? How could he handle her oxygen? What if something were to happen at home? It was a relief that they agreed to let her stay the weekend, but I was not stopping yet.

I did some online research into NYU (New York University). A ton of information came up on a great oncologist who specialized in lung cancer and I knew they did more advanced treatments that may be able to save Mom's life, or at least prolong it so I would have more time with her.

Again I went to the hospitals x-ray unit and collected copies of all Mom's x-rays, had them shipped to NYU along with a picture of

Mom's beautiful face and a brief summary of Mom's situation, begging for help. I even got her oncologist to call him and see if he would take the case. Now by this point it was Sunday afternoon. We would have to wait until he receives her records on Tuesday morning to find out if they would accept her case.

THE BEGINNING OF THE END

It was May 27th 2013, Memorial Day. Any other Memorial Day weekend I would be partying with friends, celebrating life, drink in hand, good music on, and tons of dancing. Not this Memorial Day. I spent all weekend at Morristown Memorial Hospital with Mom. I didn't want to leave her side. Several people came to visit her, my friends, her friends, and family members.

She kept asking me "So what are you doing for Memorial Day? Why aren't you down the shore? Why aren't you out with your friends?" I looked at her and said "Mom, there is nowhere else in the world I would rather be right now than right here with you."

She begged the nurse to let her wash her hair, finally the nurse gave in. My older sister, Kristina, helped her. Clumps of hair were falling out from the chemotherapy treatments she had a few days prior. She never lost her hair from any chemotherapy treatments before, so this was new to us. I remember Mom asking "is my hair falling out?" with tears in her eyes. She rarely cried in front of us. She was strong, positive, determined, & had a great will to live. Even with the tears she held back, she still had a smile on her face.

In this moment of sadness, I sat there and stared at the wall thinking to myself "how could this be my life? Why me? Why her? What did she do to deserve this?" My beautiful 47 year old mother was in the hospital dying from stage 4 non-small cell lung cancer that had spread to her bones. Yes she was a smoker, but she quit 4 years before she was diagnosed. What does it matter if she was a smoker? It's still my mother, she's still dying from this terrible disease, and the past can't be changed. Besides, the type of lung cancer she had is found in those of non-smokers.

I was so very hopeful that NYU was going to take her case. One more day, one more day I kept telling myself. Be patient, be patient. Mom really wasn't too talkative. Me, Dad, Kristina and Dawn hung out with her for a while, mostly watching the monitors and trying to make her smile. But Mom was so tired and in so much pain.

Even though we would have to wait one more day to hear from NYU, I decided in my own mind that they were in fact going to take her and I should go home and prepare for the week ahead in the city. I gave Mom a hug and left the hospital.

I went home and started to pre-cook meals for Dad for the week ahead, I knew we'd be doing a lot of running around. I remember so clearly that I was making hard boiled eggs, and there was a glass by the stove, it shattered in pieces, I'm still not sure why that happened. Seconds later my phone rang. It was about 9:45 pm. It was Dawn, she and Dad were still at the hospital with Mom. Dawn was very calm when I answered the phone. She said "Jen, why don't you come back to the hospital, Mom's heart rate is very high, were not too sure what's going on but just come." I immediatcly got in my car in a panic. I must have called dawn back 15 times to get updates.

I drove the 40 minutes or so to the hospital fearing the worst. When I arrived at the hospital Kristina, Dawn, and Danielle were all there along with Dad in the family waiting room. Mom was in the Medical ICU unit. Dad and Kristina went into the room first to check on Mom, they only allowed two people in at a time. Dawn told me to go in the room, I was really hesitant, but I took Dawns advice and went in.

Just as I was walking into Mom's hospital room the cardiologist was speaking with Dad and Kristina, explaining to them that Mom was having heart failure and they could either do a procedure to see where the blockage was or try to treat her medically. The doctor went on explaining that if they attempt the procedure she most likely won't make it. Dad decided on trying to treat her medically.

I went in the room and saw Mom, she was very confused and out of it, she kept putting her hand up to her forehead as if she were hot. She was very pale. I left the room to collect myself; I took a little walk down the hall and paced back and forth for a few minutes. I still wasn't sure what was going on. I went back into the room and grabbed Mom's hand, it was ice cold, and in that moment I realized what was happening.

I squeezed Mom's hand and looked her straight in the eyes; I told her that I loved her so much. She looked at me, nodded her head and gave a slight smile; almost as if she couldn't speak but was acknowledging that she knew what I said.

She didn't even have to say "I love you too"; the look on her face said exactly how much she loved me.

The monitors in the room started going off and I recall looking at the screen, her blood pressure was dangerously low and her heart rate was dangerously high. I ran out of the room, it was more than I could bare.

I ran down the hallway almost to the waiting room, and not even a minute later I heard the flat line of the heart monitor. I heard Kristina's heart breaking scream, and I saw Dawn at the end of the hall way in a panic. "Code blue! Code blue!" sounded over the hospitals loud speaker as two dozen nurses ran past me down the hall into Mom's room.

I dropped to the floor. My whole world stopped. Dad and Dawn were still in Mom's room as Kristina ran out screaming and crying. It was a panic, hectic disaster in the family waiting room, and in that very moment I knew. I knew there was nothing else they could do. I sat there and stared at the wall for a few minutes in disbelief.

At 11:53 pm on Monday, May 27th, 2013, Memorial Day, Mom became an angel. After her ten month battle with lung cancer, my brave, beautiful, strong, loving mother was taken from this world at the young age of 48.

FREE BIRD

Dad finally came out of Mom's hospital room; I could see him walking down the long hallway to the waiting room. The look of sadness in his eyes was overwhelming. He had just lost the love of his life and I had just lost my best friend. Everyone who knew her lost a part of their heart that night.

I couldn't bring myself to go back into the room to say my final goodbyes to Mom; I didn't have that same strength that she carried with her every day. And I didn't want to remember her like that. It would only be here body that would be there, her soul had already flown away with the angels. And I had to be okay with that.

I believe that certain events are meant to happen at an exact Moment, and I believe I was meant to walk out of that room right before

Mom died. I don't think I could go on if I saw something like that. Especially involving my own mother.

It was pretty late, probably 2 am, by the time we gathered up the strength to leave the hospital. I didn't want to leave; it felt like I was leaving her behind. I didn't want to go home and go to bed. I knew waking up the next morning was going to be one of the hardest things I'd ever have to do. To realize that it wasn't a nightmare and Mom really is gone.

We all walked out of the hospital together, it was a very quiet and sad moment. We were maybe three steps out of the hospital when I heard a strange noise. It was a bird up in a huge tree; it was the loudest bird I have ever heard. We all looked at each other and said how weird it was that a bird was being that loud that late at night.

I looked up at the huge tree and there was a twig shaped into a cancer ribbon at the very top. I got this sense over me, this sense that it was Mom. I took out my cell phone and recorded a short video of the bird chirping so loudly. As I was walking away from the tree which I so badly did not want to leave. I yelled "I love you Mom." As I watched the video back, a tiny orb shaped into a smiling face was at the bottom of the video.

To this day I believe that was Mom's way of telling us she is finally free of the cancer, free of the pain, and free as a bird.

May 28th, 2013- My Facebook post the morning after Mom died.

"With the heaviest heart I am so sad to say heaven gained a new angel. Last night my beautiful mother lost her ten month battle with lung cancer. I love you Mom, words can never describe how much you will be missed, and my life will just never be the same without you in it. I am so thankful I got to spend every minute I could for the past 10 months right by your side so you knew you were never alone. We love you more than you'll ever know. Calling all angels."

TREASURES FROM HEAVEN

The next few days were the hardest days of my life. I was in shock; I couldn't believe Mom was really gone. Each morning I woke up crying.

As we prepared the poster picture boards for Mom's celebration of life, Dad came down the stairs and said he had found a letter from Mom!

The letter read-

"To Bob, Kristina, & Jenna,

When you see butterflies & lady bugs, it will be me watching over you all. Tell your kids how much I loved them even before they were born. Dad will make a great grandpa someday. I will watch over my family. I love you all"

Along with that letter, I found a wish bone in a box, it was left from Mom. The note said

"Make a wish, I love you"

Another treasure I found was a poem from Mom to me and Kristina. The poem explained the bond between a mother and daughter and at the end in Mom's handwriting it read:

"I love you both so very much! No matter what I will always be with you! Forever until we meet again.

Love, Mom"

Months after Mom passed away, Dad went to go deactivate her e-mail account because it was sending spam out to several people. Right before clicking the deactivate button, he found an email from Mom dated

February 12, 2013. The subject of the email was "Read when I go bye bye…"

Even after her death she still continues to make us laugh. Who writes that? Shouldn't it be something more along the lines of "Read when I am no longer here" but not Mom, she always had to make it a funny situation, and I love her even more for that.

The e-mail was her final thoughts and goodbyes separately to each one of her closest friends and family members.

I could recall clearly I was in the grocery store about to check out; that e-mail had been forwarded to me from Dad. I didn't know what it was when I opened it, but soon realized. Mom's section to me read…

"Dear Jenna, wow you have come a long way. I am so proud of you. You have

become a very strong willed woman. I worry about you even though I know you always do the right thing. You have so many people that love you and care for you like a mother. You're very lucky. I will always be with you, forever in your heart and mind. I want you to tell your kids how much I loved them even before they were born. You're my little mini me. I was so blessed to have you in my life. Stay close to Danielle and Kristina. Be the best you can be and always learn from your past. I love you very much. You're some kind of wonderful, yes you are <3 Love, Mom"

"Some Kind of Wonderful", **Wow** does that bring back memories. Memories I will hold in my heart forever. Since as far back as I could remember Mom and I would hear that song and dance around her bedroom.

Whenever one of us heard it on the radio we would call each other screaming into the phone "guess what song is on!!" and we both always knew what it was.

I often read these letters she left behind, they make me smile. I realize how truly blessed I am, blessed beyond words. I will have these for the rest of my life, to show my children someday so they can get an idea of who Mom was. But when I do read them I also can't help but wonder what was going through Mom's mind when she wrote these notes.

A few days before Mom died she had given me an air freshener for my car, the kind that dangles from your rearview mirror. Now that I think about it, I don't even know where she got it from or why she had it with her. I was still driving that trusty old rental car that I had been given from my accident, so I put the air freshener in a safe place until I could get my car back.

The morning after Mom died I got a phone call telling me my car was all fixed and ready for pick up and they apologized for taking so long. Nearly a month!

I got into my car, hung the air freshener Mom gave me and It had writing on it. It read "There is an angel watching over you." I thought to myself what a coincidence that I got my car back the day after Mom died, and the air freshener she gave me had those words written on it. I took that as a sign, a sign that my angel will always watch over me, no matter what.

CELEBRATING A BEAUTIFUL LIFE

June 1st, 2013. It was a beautiful summer day, the weather was perfect. I can remember waking up that morning with the worst anxiety. I couldn't believe I was going to a memorial service for my own mother. This can't be real! She was only 48. I am only 24. This doesn't make sense to me.

Even though I dread public speaking, I decided I was going to do a speech for Mom. I had to, if I didn't I knew I would have so much regret.

Mom was never an overly religious person. She had her own beliefs, just like everybody else. But I did know that she believed in god and angels. She talked to me about it before. She believed that when you die you are reunited with the ones you love. And because of her I now believe that too.

Mom would always joke with me, even before we found out she was sick, she would say "When I die I do not want everybody standing there crying, I want a celebration. I want people to be happy when remembering me. I want good music playing and I want shots of patron being passed around!" I would always look at her and say "Oh Mom, you're one of a kind, that's for sure! And besides you're not going anywhere for a while so stop saying that!" We would both laugh. Unfortunately I found out sooner than later that she did in fact want this type of memorial. She absolutely did not want a funeral, and no church service. She wanted a celebration. Her main wish was to be cremated and made into a necklace. She wanted me, my sister, my grandmother, and my cousins to all have a necklace of our choice with her ashes in it. And we made sure that wish was fulfilled. I got a beautiful silver dove necklace. I can now wear it every day, close to my heart just where she belongs. The urn we picked for her was her favorite color deep purple, with "Our Angel" engraved on it.

Her memorial service started around 1 or 2 pm, the funeral home was flooded with hundreds of people, the place was packed wall to wall and out the doors. I knew a lot of people would come, but I didn't realize it would be that many. It was a true testament of what kind of heart she had. She was so loved by many.

We started the speeches, one of Mom's friends went first, then Mom's childhood best friend went, my best friend Joelle who was like a daughter to Mom was up next, and then it was my cousin Danielle's turn. Danielle was Mom's god daughter and Mom loved her and cared for her so much. Danielle's speech was beautiful along with all of them.

It was suddenly my turn, the moment I was dreading. I wasn't sure how I would get through my speech without balling my eyes out. I went up to the podium, took a deep breath, looked over at Mom's urn & beautiful picture next to me and I started my speech.

"24 years ago I laid eyes on one of the best people to ever step foot on this earth. I can't put into words the love she had for her family and friends. She brought joy to many, whether it was for a minute or for a lifetime. She was and always will be an inspiration to so many people. Despite the fact that she had a terminal cancer, she still always put others first. When she was first diagnosed, she did not look at it as a death sentence. She looked at it as more of a reason to go out there and live the life she loved. She never judged anyone; she always saw the good in every person she met. She was the perfect wife to my Dad, a loving mother to me, my sister and her god daughter Danielle, an amazing cousin and a supportive friend. She will one day be an amazing grandma from heaven. She was a simple person with a simple life; she never asked for much, all she wanted was more time with the people she loved so deeply. She taught me to always be kind to others and to treat people exactly the way I want to be treated, and that I will carry with me forever. She is free of pain now & has flown away with the angels. Mom, we will be counting down the days until we get to see you again, I love you."

After my speech I had played a song, a song that I heard the day after she passed away, a song that I hold very dear in my heart now. The lyrics sang out "You're my back bone, you're my corner stone, you're my crutch when my legs stop moving, you're my head start, you're my rugged heart, you're the pulse that I've always needed. Like a drum baby don't stop beating, like a drum baby don't stop beating, like a drum my heart never stops beating for you. And long after you're gone, I'll love you long after you're gone, gone, gone….." (Phillip Phillips- "Gone, gone, gone")

Everyone clapped. I saw smiling faces and I saw many teary eyes. I knew in that moment that everything I had just said, in just a few short minutes, summed up Mom's life exactly.

We finished up, gathered all of the pictures and posters that hung. I grabbed my playlist of music that we had playing, and the CD of pictures that displayed on TV screens throughout the funeral home. We had another celebration after, but this was the real type of celebration Mom wanted. We had food, music, shots, and drinks. There was about 80 close friends and family members there. We all talked about Mom, shared stories and laughed.

We later released several purple balloons and sent them up to our sweet angel in heaven. I went home with a warm heart knowing Mom was smiling down and her all of her final wishes were fulfilled.

I was amazed by my own strength that day. I made it through the whole speech without crying, and that is because I know she was sending me her strength, she was right there by my side, just like she will always be for the rest of my time on this earth.

FINDING MY NEW NORMAL

"There is an emptiness inside me—a void that will never be filled. No one in your life will ever love you as your mother does. There is no love as pure, unconditional and strong as a mother's love. And I will never be loved that way again."

-Hope Edelman (Motherless Daughters)

Before Mom was diagnosed I couldn't say I was the best person I could be. I wasn't always kind to others, and I wasn't always the most positive person in the world.

I truly believe that through these heart breaking yet life changing moments, I was starting to become the amazing woman that Mom always had been. I found an inner strength to go on; I found a new reason to live. The reason was her. All she ever wanted was for me to be happy. So that's what I was going to do. Be happy.

If it weren't for cancer, I would say I have the perfect life. But then again if it weren't for cancer, would I even realize it?

Everybody around me knew Mom was gone. But they didn't really know. They didn't really know the pain and heartache it caused. They didn't really know how much I truly missed her.

I had to try to get back into my normal routine, but it almost seemed as if I was betraying Mom, it seemed wrong. Every time I remembered that she was no longer here, it was like a shock to my heart. Almost as if she had died over and over again each and every day. Everything that was to come into my life and everything I will do for the rest of my life would only make it one more day that we would be further apart. Or maybe it was one more day closer until the day I get to be with her again.

They say time heals all wounds, but I don't believe that to be true. I believe that time has a funny way of making you forget, and time has a way of moving so fast that you have no choice but to move on, but some wounds can never be fully healed. Especially wounds that leave you broken hearted. Ultimately it is what you do while the time passes is what will make all the difference.

THE WORLD AROUND US

I often look back at particular events in life and wonder if certain people are placed into your life for a reason, if certain things happen to prepare you for what's to come. Once you are born, is your life already planned out for you? Can you really fight fate or is everything just one big coincidence?

I truly believe that what you see in the world around you is a reflection of who you are. Positivity plays a big part in life. You can spend life feeling sorry for yourself for unfortunate burdens that have come your way, or you can collect yourself and move on. Move on to be a stronger person, a better person, a person that you would want to know.

The past can't be changed nor is it made to be. You cannot dwell on what already has come and gone but you can control how you will your future will turn out. You can control it with a certain mind set, you must set yourself up for the worst, so when the worst comes you're prepared. But never give up on hope.

I think we sometimes get so caught up in lives busy moments that we forget to stop and think about the simple things. The phone calls to an old friend, telling someone how much you truly love them and the simple walks around your neighborhood. I don't think we forget about these moments on purpose, I just think we assume these moments and opportunities will never be taken away. This is why we must walk slower, open our eyes so we don't miss all the great things that are passing by.

Some days I feel I've lost my way, I get off track of where I want to be. I force myself to find the strength to keep on going, just like Mom did. Though she is no longer physically here on earth, I do believe that she sends me her strength. The same strength she used to hide her pain, the same strength she used to make others smile even while her own heart was breaking, and for me that is an irreplaceable gift that Mom has given me, and it could never be taken away.

LIFE GOES ON

"Time moves on for us, but for you it stands still. You will be forever ageless, as we grow old. Your smile will never wrinkle. Nor will that beautiful Shine in your eyes ever fade."

-Kendal Rob

Weeks went by, the weeks turned into months. Day by day everything started to change. These days slowly started to turn into my "new normal." The summer following Mom's passing, butterflies followed me everywhere. I was given a butterfly bush by a co-worker; we planted it near the house. Along with the butterfly bush was a note. It read "Look for that special butterfly, the one that keeps on coming back." And there was one very pretty one that always returned. I like to think that was Mom popping in to check on us every now and again.

I went to the Train concert that July and the first song they sang was Mom's song, "Calling all angels." I remember looking to the sky and wondering if she was there with me, singing along. I could almost feel her presence right next to me as tears fell down my cheeks.

We celebrated Mom's 49th birthday, but this time she wasn't here to celebrate with us. We wrote notes attached to balloons and sent them up to our angel in heaven.

Thanksgiving and Christmas flew by. It was not the same without her, we tried to stick to the traditions, but we all missed Mom so very much. I had a Christmas ornament made in Mom's memory. It was a beautiful heart with doves and hand written on it was, "All hearts come home for Christmas, Our Beautiful Angel, Gina."

The New Year came, the first New Year ever without Mom by my side. I remembered the statue that I had given Mom the year before, "Every day is a gift, each year a new beginning." It was a new beginning, the beginning of a new life for me. And each day is a certainly is gift.

I experienced most of the firsts without Mom. I celebrated my 25th birthday as her one year "Angelversary" quickly approached; I look back and realize how far I've come, and how much further I will go.

May 27th, 2014 was the last of the firsts without Mom here on earth and in a weird way I never wanted the firsts without her to end, but just as Mom always said....

Life Goes On.

For My Mother,

Gina Marie Lowthert

October 30th 1964 – May 27th 2013

May the Angels Lead You Home.

I Love You More.

Made in United States
Orlando, FL
08 June 2022

18599940R00093